Tales of Cornish Giants

Robert Hunt

Bossiney Books • Exeter

Robert Hunt

Robert Hunt (1807-1887) was a scientist and poet, born in Devonport. His father was a naval officer who drowned while Robert was still a child. He studied as a chemist in London, but became ill in 1828, and moved back to convalesce in Cornwall, where he gathered folk-lore tales.

In 1840 he was appointed secretary to the Royal Cornwall Polytechnic Society in Falmouth, then became keeper of mining records at the Museum of Economic Geology in London, where he also lectured.

At the same time he was an early pioneer of photography, publishing *A Manual of Photography* in 1841, and wrote poetry. In 1865 he published *Popular Romances of the West of England or the drolls, traditions and superstitions of old Cornwall*, based on his own research and that of Thomas Quiller Couch and William Bottrell. The present book is entirely drawn from this source. Minor editorial changes have been made, in particular to place-name spellings.

First published 2023 by
Bossiney Books Ltd,
68 Thorndale Courts, Whitycombe Way, Exeter, Devon, EX4 2NY
www.bossineybooks.com
ISBN 978-1-915664-18-1

Acknowledgements
Cover artwork by Beth Paisley

Printed in Great Britain by Deltor, Saltash, Cornwall

Corineus and Gogmagog

Who can dare question such an authority as John Milton?

In his *History of Britain, that part especially now called England. From the first Traditional beginning continued to the Norman Conquest. Collected out of the antientest and best authors thereof* he gives us the story of Brutus and of Corineus, 'who with the battele Ax which he was wont to manage against the Tyrrhen Giants, is said to have done marvells.'

With the adventures of these heroes in Africa and in Aquitania we have little concern. They suffer severe defeats; and then 'Brutus, finding now his powers much lessn'd, and this not yet the place foretold him, leaves Aquitain, and with an easy course arriving at Totness in Devonshire, quickly perceivs heer to be the promis'd end of his labours.'

The following matters interest us more closely:

> The Land, not yet Britain, but Albion, was in a manner desert and inhospitable, kept only by a remnant of Giants, whose excessive Force and Tyrannie had consumed the rest. Them Brutus destroies, and to his people divides the land, which, with some reference to his own name, he thenceforth calls Britain. To Corineus, Cornwall, as now we call it, fell by lot; the rather by him lik't, for that the hugest Giants in Rocks and Caves were said to lurk still there; which kind of Monsters to deal with was his old exercise.

> And heer, with leave bespok'n to recite a grand fable, though dignify'd by our best Poets: While Brutus, on a certain Festival day, solemnly kept on that shoar where he first landed (Totness) was with the People in great jollity and mirth, a crew of these savages, breaking in upon them, began on the sudden another sort of Game than at such a meeting was expected. But at length by many hands overcome, Goemagog, the hugest, in hight twelve cubits, is reserved alive; that with him Corineus, who desired nothing more, might try his strength, whom in a Wrestle the Giant catching aloft, with a terrible hugg broke three of his Ribs:

3

Nevertheless Corineus, enraged, heaving him up by main force, and on his shoulders bearing him to the next high rock, threw him hedlong all shatter'd into the sea, and left his name on the cliff, called ever since Langoetnagog, which is to say, the Giant's Leap.

The same story has been somewhat differently told, although there is but little variation in the main incidents. When Brutus and Corineus, with their Trojan hosts, landed at Plymouth, these chiefs wisely sent parties into the interior to explore the country, and to learn something of the people. At the end of the first day, all the soldiers who had been sent out as exploring parties, returned in great terror, pursued by several terrific giants. Brutus and Corineus were not, however, to be terrified by the immense size of their enemies, nor by the horrid noises which they made, hoping to strike terror into the armed hosts.

These chieftains rallied their hosts and marched to meet the giants, hurling their spears and flinging their darts against their huge bodies. The assault was so unexpected that the giants gave way, and eventually fled to the hills of Dartmoor. Gogmagog, the captain of the giants, who was sadly wounded in the leg, and, unable to proceed, hid himself in a bog; but there, by the light of the moon, he was found by the Trojan soldiers, bound with strong cords, and carried back to the Hoe at Plymouth, where the camp was. Gogmagog was treated nobly by his victors, and his wounds were speedily healed. Brutus desired to make terms with the giants; and it was at length proposed by Gogmagog to try a fall with the strongest in the host, and that whoever came off the conqueror should be proclaimed king of Cornwall, and hold possession of all the western land. Corineus at once accepted the challenge of the monster. Notwithstanding, the giant,

Though bent with woes,
Full eighteen feet in height he rose;
His hair, exposed to sun and wind,
Like wither'd heath, his head entwined,

4

and that Corineus was but little above the ordinary size of man, the Trojan chief felt sure of a victory. The day for the wrestling was fixed. The huge Gogmagog was allowed to send for the giants, and they assembled on one side of a cleared space on Plymouth Hoe, while the Trojan soldiers occupied the other. All arms were thrown aside; and fronting each other, naked to the waist, stood the most lordly of the giants, and the most noble of men.

The conflict was long, and it appeared for some time doubtful. Brute strength was exerted on one side, and trained skill on the other. At length Corineus succeeded in seizing Gogmagog by the girdle, and by regularly repeated impulses he made the monster undulate like a tree shaken by a winter storm, until at length, gathering all his strength into one effort, the giant was forced to his back on the ground, the earth shaking with his weight, and the air echoing with the thunder of his mighty groan, as the breath was forced from his body by the terrible momentum of his fall. There lay the giant, and there were all the other giants, appalled at the power which they could not understand, but which convinced them that there was something superior to mere animal strength.

Corineus breathed for a minute, then he rushed upon his prostrate foe, and seizing him by the legs, he dragged him to the edge of the cliff, and precipitated him into the sea. The giant fell on the rocks below, and his body was broken into fragments by the fall; while the

Fretted flood
Roll'd frothy waves of purple blood.

'Gogmagog's Leap' has been preserved near the spot which now presents a fortress to the foes of Britain; and there are those 'who say that, at the last digging on the Haw for the foundation of the citadel of Plymouth, the great jaws and teeth therein found were those of Gogmagog.'

The Giants of the Mount

The history of the redoubtable Jack proves that St Michael's Mount was the abode of the giant Cormelian, or, as the name is sometimes given, Cormoran. We are told how Jack destroyed the giant, and the story ends. Now, the interesting part, which has been forgotten in the narrative, is not only that Cormoran lived on, but that he built the Mount, his dwelling-place.

St Michael's Mount, as is tolerably well known, is an island at each rise of the tide – the distance between it and the mainland being a little more than a quarter of a mile. In the days of the giants, however, it was some six miles from the sea, and was known as the White Rock in the Wood, or in Cornish, *Carreg luz en kuz*. In this wood the giant desired to build his home, and to rear it above the trees, that he might from the top keep watch over the neighbouring country.

Any person carefully observing the structure of the granite rocks will notice their tendency to a cubical form. These stones were carefully selected by the giant from the granite of the neighbouring hills, and he was for a long period employed in carrying and piling those huge masses, one on the other, in which labour he compelled his wife to aid him. It has been suggested, with much show of probability, that the confusion of the two names alluded to has arisen from the fact that the giant was called Cormoran, and that the name of his wife was Cormelian; at all events, there is no harm in adopting this hypothesis.

The toil of lifting those granitic masses from their primitive beds, and of carrying them through the forest, was excessive. It would seem that the heaviest burthens were imposed upon Cormelian, and that she was in the habit of carrying those rocky masses in her apron. At a short distance from the White Rock, which was now approaching completion, there exist large masses of greenstone rock. Cormelian saw no reason why one description of stone would not do as well as another; and one day, when the giant Cormoran was sleeping, she broke off a vast mass of the greenstone rock, and taking it in her apron, hastened towards the artificial hill with it, hoping to place it without being observed by Cormoran.

When, however, Cormelian was within a short distance of the White Rock, the giant awoke, and presently perceived that his wife was, contrary to his wishes, carrying a green stone instead of a white one. In great wrath he arose, followed her, and, with a dreadful imprecation, gave her a kick. Her apron-string broke, and the stone fell on the sand. There it has ever since remained, no human power being sufficient to remove it. The giantess died, and the mass of greenstone, resting, as it does, on clay slate rocks, became her monument.

In more recent days, when the light of Christianity was dawning on the land, this famous rock was still rendered sacred, 'a lytle chapel' having been built on it; and to this day it is usually known as the 'The Chapel Rock'.

The Key of the Giant's Castle

The giant's castle at Treryn, remarkable as a grand example of truly British Cyclopean architecture, was built by the power of enchantment. The giant to whom all the rest of his race were indebted for this stronghold was in every way a remarkable mortal. He was stronger than any other giant, and he was a mighty necromancer. He sat on the promontory of Treryn, and by the power of his will he compelled the castle to rise out of the sea. It is only kept in its present position by virtue of a magic key. This the giant placed in a holed rock, known as the Giant's Lock, and whenever this key, a large round stone, can be taken out of the lock, the promontory of Treryn and its castle will disappear beneath the waters. There are not many people who obtain even a sight of this wonderful key. You must pass at low tide along a granite ledge, scarcely wide enough for a goat to stand on. If you happen to make a false step, you must be dashed to pieces on the rocks below. Well, having got over safely, you come to a pointed rock with a hole in it; this is the castle lock.

Put your hand deep into the hole, and you will find at the bottom a large egg-shaped stone, which is easily moved in any direction. You will feel certain that you can take it out – but try! Try as you may, you will find it will not pass through the hole; yet no one can doubt but that it once went in.

Lieutenant Goldsmith dissolved one bit of superstition by foolishly throwing the fatal Logan Stone from off its bearing; but no one has ever yet succeeded in removing the key of the giant's castle from the hole in which the necromancer is said to have placed it when he was dying.

The Rival Giants

Those who have visited the Logan Rock will be familiar with the several groups which form the Treryn promontory. Treryn Castle, an ancient British fortress, the Cyclopean walls of which, and its outer earthwork, can still be traced, was the dwelling of a famous giant and his wife. I have heard it said that he gave his name to this place, but that is, of course, doubtful. This giant was chief of a numerous band, and by his daring he held possession, against the giants of the Mount, of all the lands west of Penzance.

Amongst the hosts who owned allegiance to him, was a remarkable fine young fellow, who had his abode in a cave, in the pile of rocks upon which the Logan Rock stands. This young giant grew too fond of the giantess, and it would appear that the lady was not unfavourably inclined towards him. Of their love passes, however, we know nothing. Tradition has only told us that the giantess was one day reclining on the rock still known as the Giant Lady's Chair, while the good old giant was dosing in the Giant's Chair which stands near it, when the young and wicked lover stole behind his chief and stabbed him in the belly with a knife. The giant fell over the rocks to the level ridge below, and there he lay, rapidly pouring out his life-blood. From this spot the young murderer kicked him into the sea, ere yet his life was quite extinct, and he perished in the waters.

The guilty pair took possession of Treryn Castle, and, we are told, lived happily for many years.

The Giants of Trencrom or Trecobben

The rough granite hill of Trecrobben rises in almost savage grandeur from the wooded lands which form the park of Trevetha, close by the picturesque village of Lelant. From the summit of this hill may be surveyed one of the most striking panoramic views in Cornwall. The country declines, rather rapidly, but still with a pleasing contour, towards the sea on the southern side. From the sandy plain, which extends from Marazion to Penzance, there stretch out two arms of land, one on the eastern side, towards the Lizard Point, and the other on the western side towards Mousehole and Lamorna, which embrace as it were that fine expanse of water known as the Mount's Bay.

The most striking object, 'set in the silver sea', is the pyramidical hill St Michael's Mount, crowned with the 'castle', an unhappy mixture of church, castle, and modern dwelling-house, which, nevertheless, from its very incongruities, has a picturesque appearance when viewed from a distance. Nestling amidst the greenstone rocks, sheltered by 'the Holy Mount', is the irregular town of Marazion, or Market-Jew; and, balancing this, on the western side of 'the Green', Penzance displays her more important buildings, framed by the beautifully fertile country by which the town is surrounded.

The high lands to the westward of Penzance, with the fishing villages of Newlyn and Mousehole, the church of Paul on the summit of the hill, and the engine-house belonging to a mine at its base, have much quiet beauty under some aspects of light – the yet more western hills shutting out the Land's End from the observer's eye.

Looking from Trencrom (this is the more common name) to the south-east, the fine hills of Tregonning and Godolphin – which have given names to two ancient Cornish families – mark the southern boundary of a district famed for its mineral wealth. Looking eastward, Carn Brea Hill, with its ancient castle and its modern monument, stands up from the tableland in rugged grandeur. This hill, 'a merry place, 'tis said, in days of yore' – when British villages were spread amidst the mighty cairns, and Cyclopean walls sheltered the inhabitants – rises to mark the most productive piece of mining-ground, of the same area, to be found in the world. Around the towns of Camborne and Redruth are seen hundreds of miners' cottages, and scores of tall chimneys, telling of the mechanical appliances which are brought to bear upon the extraction of tin and copper from the earth. Beyond this thickly-peopled region the eye wanders yet eastward, and eventually reposes on the series of granite hills which rise beyond St Austell and stretch northward – the two highest hills in Cornwall, which are known as Roughtor and Brown Willy being in this range.

Let the observer now turn his face northward, and a new and varied scene lies before him. Within two miles the waters of St Ives Bay break against the cliffs. On the left is the creek of Hayle, which has been fashioned by the energy of man into a useful harbour, and given rise to the foundation of two extensive iron-foundries. Between those and the sea are the hills of blown sand, which have ever been the homes of the Fairy people. The lighthouse of Godrevy stands, a humble companion, to balance in this bay the Mount, which adorns the bay, wasting the southern slope of this narrow neck of land. Godrevy marks the region of sand extending to the eastward. To the north the shores become more and more rugged, culminating in St Agnes Beacon – a hill of graceful form rising somewhat rapidly to a considerable elevation. From this the 'beetling cliffs' stretch away northward, until the bold promontory Trevose Head closes the scene, appropriately displaying another of those fine examples of humanity – a lighthouse.

To the left, towards the sea, rises the cenotaph of Knill, an eccentric man, who evidently sought to secure some immortality by this building, and the silly ceremonials carried on around it;

the due performance of which he has secured by bequests to the Corporation of St Ives. Around this the mining district of St Ives is seen, and her fishing-boats dotting the sea give evidence of another industry of vast importance to the town and neighbourhood. Westward of St Ives, hills more brown and rugged than any which have yet been viewed stretch away to Zennor, Morvah, and St Just, and these, girding the scene beneath our feet, shut out from us the region of the Land's End.

On the summit of this hill, which is only surpassed in savage grandeur by Carn Brea, the giants built a castle – the four entrances to which still remain in Cyclopean massiveness to attest the Herculean powers by which such mighty blocks were piled upon each other. There the giant chieftains dwelt in awful state. Along the serpentine road, passing up the hill to the principal gateway, they dragged their captives, and on the great flat rocks within the castle they sacrificed them. Almost every rock still bears some name connected with the giants – 'a race may perish, but the name endures'.

The treasures of the giants who dwelt here are said to have been buried in the days of their troubles, when they were perishing before the conquerors of their land. Their gold and jewels were hidden deep in the granite caves of this hill, and secured by spells as potent as those which Merlin placed upon his hoarded treasures. They are securely preserved, even to the present day, and carefully guarded from man by the Spriggans, or Trolls.

The Giants at Play

In several parts of Cornwall there are evidences that these Titans were a sportive race. Huge rocks are preserved to show where they played at trap-ball, at hurling, and other athletic games. The giants of Trecrobben and St Michael's Mount often met for a game at bob-buttons. The Mount was the 'bob', on which flat masses of granite were placed to serve as buttons, and Trecrobben Hill was the 'mit', or the spot from which the throw was made. This order was sometimes reversed. On the outside of St Michael's Mount, many a granite slab which had been knocked off the bob is yet to be found; and numerous piles of rough cubical masses of the same rock, said to be the granite of Trecrobben Hill, show how eagerly the game was played.

Trecrobben Hill was well chosen by the giants as the site of their castle. From it they surveyed the country on every side; and friend or enemy was seen at a considerable distance as he approached the guarded spot. It is as clear as tradition can make it, that Trecrobben was the centre of a region full of giants.

On Lescudjack Hill, close to Penzance, there is 'The Giant's Round', evidently the scene of many a sanguinary conflict, since the Cornish antiquarian authority Borlase informs us, that Lesgudzhek signifies the 'Castle of the Bloody Field'. On the cairn at Gulval are several impressions on the rocks, all referable to the giants. In Madron there is the celebrated 'Giant's Cave'; and the well-known Lanyon cromlech is reported by some to be the 'Giant's Coit', while others declare it to be the 'Giant's Table'. Cairn Galva, again, is celebrated for its giant; and, indeed, every hill within sight has some monument preserving the memory of those, 'the Titans fierce'.

Holiburn of the Cairn

Holiburn, according to tradition, was a very amiable and somewhat sociable gentleman; but, like his brethren, he loved to dwell amongst the rocks of Cairn Galva. He made his home in this remote region, and relied for his support on the gifts of sheep and oxen from the farmers around – he, in return, protecting them from the predatory incursions of the less conscientious giants of Trecrobben. It is said that he fought many a battle in the defence of his friends, and that he injured but one of his neighbours during his long lifetime. This was, however, purely an accident. The giant was at play with the human pigmies, and in the excitement of the moment, being delighted at the capital game made by a fine young peasant, he tapped him on the head, and scattered his brains on the grass. I once heard that Holiburn had married a farmer's daughter, and that a very fine race, still bearing a name not very dissimilar, was the result of this union.

Holiburn, like his brethren, was remarkably fond of quoits; indeed, go where we will within the Land's End district, the 'Giant's Quoit' is still shown.

Other – shall we call them household? – relics of the giants occur. From Cairn Galva to Zennor we find a series of 'Giant's Chairs'; and, careful to preserve each remarkable relic of this interesting race, here is also the 'Giant's Dinner-plate'. That St Ives, too, was not without its giant, although the record of his name is lost, is evident from the fact that a tooth, an inch broad, was taken from a 'Giant's Grave'.

The following extract from a note written by the late Zennor postman and poet, shows how enduringly the giants have left their names on the rocks of Cornwall:

> Some districts in Cornwall were said to have been peopled in olden times by giants, and even Zennor district possesses the largest quoit – three Logan rocks – whilst Trecrobben Hill still exhibits the bowl in which the giants of the west used to wash. The large granite boulder near to the residence of the Rev. Mr S, curate of Morvah, is said to be the Giant's Dinner-plate. Farther down the hill, and hard by the Zennor vicarage, the seats of the giants are still shown by the inhabitants. Indeed, so strong is the belief that giants inhabited the hills of the west, that a young lady in this neighbourhood assayed, a month or two ago, to deliver a lecture, or address, on the subject, taking for her text, 'There were giants in those days.' But the giants were not immortal; colossal as were their frames, they too had to 'sleep with their fathers'.

Whether Jack the Giant-killer took any part in ridding the earth of this wonderful race of men we cannot positively state; but thus much is certain, the giants were succeeded by a numerous race of small people, and so small as not to be observable by the eye.

The Giant of Nancledry

In Nancledry Bottoms, about a mile from the famous hill Castle-an-Dinas, there stood at one time a thatched house near the brook which runs murmuring down the valley. Rather more than thirty years since, some mouldering 'clob ' (mud) walls, indicating the existence at one time of a large dwelling, were pointed to as the former residence of a terrible giant. He appears to have led a solitary life, and to have lived principally on little children, whom he is said to have swallowed whole. His strength was indicated by several huge masses of granite which were scattered around the Bottoms, and in the neighbouring fields. These were carried by him in his pockets, to defend himself from the giants of Trecrobben, with whom he appears to have been on unfriendly terms. This giant is noteworthy as the only one recorded who lived in a house.

Trebiggan the Giant

Trebegean [Trevegean] is the name of a village near the Land's End. This name, as we have already stated, signifies the town of the giant's grave. The giant's existence was confirmed by the discovery of a vault and some large bones in it, on this spot.

Trebiggan divides with Tregeagle the honourable immortality of being employed to frighten children into virtue. Often have I heard the unruly urchins of this neighbourhood threatened with Trebiggan. They are told that Trebiggan was a vast man, with arms so long that he could take men out of the ships passing by the Land's End, and place them on the Longships; but that sometimes he would, having had his fun with them, good-humouredly place them on board their ships or boats again. He is said to have dined every day on little children, who were generally fried on a large flat rock which stood at a little distance from his cave.

The Lord of Pengersick and the Giant of St Michael's Mount

The giant who dwelt on St Michael's Mount had grown very old, and had lost all his teeth; still he was the terror of the neighbouring villages. The horrid old monster – who had but one eye, and that one in the middle of his forehead – would, whenever he required food – which was pretty often – walk or wade across to Market-Jew, as the tide might be, select the best cow in the neighbourhood, and, swinging it over his shoulders, return to his island. This giant had often taken cattle from the Pengersick estate; and one day he thought he should like another of this choice breed.

Accordingly, away he went, across the sea, to Pengersick Cove. The giant did not know that the lord of Pengersick had returned from the East, a master of 'white-witchcraft', or magic. The lord had seen the giant coming, and he began to work his spells. The giant was bewildered, yet he knew not how. At last, after much trouble, he caught a fine calf, tied its four feet together, passed his great head between the fore and hind legs, and, with the calf hanging on his shoulders, he trod in joy towards the shore.

He wandered on in perfect unconsciousness of the path, and eventually he found himself on the precipitous edge of the great black rock which still marks the western side of Pengersick Cove. As if the rock had been a magnet, the giant was chained fast. He twisted, turned, and struggled in vain. He found himself gradually becoming stiff, so that at last he could neither move hand nor foot; yet were his senses more keenly alive than ever. The giant had to remain thus, during a long winter's night, with the calf bleating, as never calf bleated before, into his ear. In the morning when the enchanter thought he had punished the giant sufficiently, he mounted his mare, and rode down to the shore. He disenchanted the giant, by giving him a severe horse-whipping, and he then made him drop the calf. He continued to flog the giant until he leaped off the rock into the sea, through which in great agony he waded to the Mount; and from that day to this he has never ventured on the mainland.

We learn, however, from undoubted authority, that some time after this, Tom, the giant of Lelant, visited the giant on the Mount, and, finding him half starved, he took his aunt Nancy from Gulval to see his friend, with a large supply of butter and eggs. The old giant was exceedingly glad to see the farmer's wife, bought all her store at a very extravagant price, and bargained and paid in advance for more. He had a store of wealth in the caverns of the Mount. The knowing old woman kept him well supplied as long as the giant had money to pay her; and aunt Nancy's family became the wealthiest in the parish of Gulval.

The Giant of St Michael's Mount loses his wife

The giant on the Mount and the giant on Trecrobben Hill were very friendly. They had only one cobbling-hammer between them, which they would throw from one to the other, as either required it. One day the giant on the Mount wanted the hammer in a great hurry, so he shouted, 'Holloa, up there! Trecrobben, throw us down the hammer, woost a'?'

'To be sure,' sings out Trecrobben; 'here! look out, and catch 'm.'

Now, nothing would do but the giant's wife, who was very near-sighted, must run out of her cave to see Trecrobben throw the hammer. She had no hat on; and coming at once out into the light, she could not distinguish objects. Consequently, she did not see the hammer coming through the air, and received it between her eyes. The force with which it was flung was so great that the massive bone of the forehead of the giantess was crushed, and she fell dead at the giant's feet. You may be sure there was a great to-do between the two giants. They sat wailing over the dead body, and with their sighs they produced a tempest. These were unavailing to restore the old lady, and all they had to do was to bury her. Some say they lifted the Chapel Rock and put her under it, others, that she is buried beneath the castle court, while some – no doubt the giants' detractors – declare that they rolled the body down into the sea, and took no more heed of it.

Tom and the Giant Blunderbuss, or
The Wheel and Exe Fight

A young giant, who does not appear to have been known by any other name than Tom, lived somewhere westward of Hayle, probably in Lelant. Tom would eat as much meat as three men, and when he was in the humour he could do as much work as half a dozen. Howbeit, Tom was a lazy fellow, and spent most of his time wandering about the parish with his hands in his pockets. Occasionally Tom would have an industrious fit; then, if he found any of his neighbours hedging, he would turn to and roll in all the largest rocks from over the fields, for 'grounders'. This was the only work Tom took delight in; he was wont to say, he could feel his strength about such work as that. Tom didn't appear so very big a man in those days, when all men were twice the size they are now. He was about four feet from shoulder to shoulder, square built, and straight all the way down from shoulder to cheens (loins).

Tom's old mother was constantly telling her idle son to do something to earn his food, but the boy couldn't find any job to his mind for a long time. At last he undertook to drive a brewer's wain, in the hope of getting into plenty of strong drink, and he went to live in Market-Jew, where the brewery was. The first day he was so employed, he was going to St Ives with his load of beer, and on the road he saw half a score of men trying to lift a fallen tree on to a 'draw'. It was, however, more than the whole of them could do.

'Stand clear!' shouts Tom. He put his hands, one on each side of the tree, and lifted it on the 'draw', without so much as saying 'Ho!' to his oxen, or looking behind him. The feat was performed in Ludgvan Lees, and a little farther on was a giant's place diverting the road, which should have gone straight to St Ives but for it. This place was hedged in with great rocks, which no ten men of these times could move. They call them the Giant's Hedges to the present day. There was a gate on that side of the giant's farm which was nearest Market-Jew, and another on that side which joined the highway leading on to St Ives. Tom looked at the gate for some time, half disposed to drive through, but eventually he decided on proceeding by the ordinary road. When, however, Tom was coming back from St Ives with his empty wain, his courage screwed up by the influence of some three or four gallons of strong beer which he had drunk, he began to reason with himself thus:

'The king's highway ought not to be twisting and turning like an angle-twitch. It should go straight through here. What right has the giant to keep his place closed, stopping honester men than he ever was longer on the road home? If everybody were of my mind, the road would soon be opened. Faith, I'll drive through. He wouldn't eat me, I suppose. My old mammy never told me I was to come to my end that way. They say the giant has had scores of wives. What becomes of them nobody can tell, yet there are always more ready to supply their place. Well, that's no business of mine. I never met the man to make me turn back yet; so come along, Neat and Comely,' shouts Tom to the oxen, opening the great gate for them to pass through.

On went Tom, without seeing anything of the giant or of anybody else, except the fat cattle of all sorts in the fields. After driving about a mile, Tom came to a pair of gates in a high wall, which was close to and surrounding the giant's castle. There was no passing round those, as deep ditches, full of water, were on either side of these gates. So at them went Tom. The huge gates creaked on their hangings, and the wheels of Tom's wain rattled on over the causey. A little ugly midgan of a cur began to bark, and out tore the giant, a great ugly unshapely fellow, all head and stomach.

'You impudent little villain,' roared the giant, 'to drive into my grounds, disturbing my afternoon's nap. What business have you here?'

'I am on the road,' says Tom, 'and you – nor a better man than you – shan't put me back. You ha' no right to build your hedges across what used to be the king's highway, and shall be again.'

'I shan't bemean myself to talk with such a little saucy blackguard as thee art,' said the giant; 'I'll get a twig, and drive thee out faster than thee came in.'

'Well,' says Tom, 'you may keep your breath to cool your porridge; but, if that's the game you are up to, I can play at that as well as you.' The giant had pulled up a young elm-tree, about twenty feet high or so, and he began stripping the small branches from the head of the tree, as he came up the hill, gaping (yawning) all the time, as if he were half asleep. Tom, seeing what he was up to, upset his wain. This he did without the oxen moving, as the tuntsy (pole) turned round in the ring of the yoke. He then slipped off the further wheel in a wink, hauled out the exe (axle-tree) fast in the other wheel, against the giant came up. (In old time the axle was made to work in gudgeons under the carts or wains.)

'Now then,' says Tom, 'fair play for the buttons. If you can beat me, I'll go back. The exe and wheel is my sword and buckler, which I'll match against your elm-tree.' Then Tom began whistling.

The giant got round the uphill side, lifted his tree, and tore towards Tom without saying a word, as if he would cleave him from head to heel. Tom lifted the axle-tree, with the wheel, up, to guard off the blow of the giant's twig – the giant being in such a towering passion to hear Tom coolly whistling all the time, that he couldn't steady himself. He missed Tom's head, struck the edge of the wheel, and, the ground being slippery, the giant fell upon his face on the ground.

Tom might have driven the 'exe' through him as he lay sprawling in the mud, and so have nailed him to the earth; but no, not he! Tom would rather be killed than not fight fair, so he just tickled the giant under the ribs with the end of the 'exe'. 'Come, get up,' says Tom, 'let 's have another turn.' The giant rose very slowly, as if he were scarcely able to stand, bent double, supporting himself on his twig. He was only dodging – the great cowardly skulk – to get the uphill side again, and take Tom unawares; but he was waiting with his right hand grasping the 'exe', the wheel resting on the ground. Quick as lightning the giant raised his tree. Tom fetched him a heavy kick on the shins, he slipped, fell forward, and Tom so held the 'exe', that it passed through his body like a spit. Good Lord, how the giant roared!

'Thee stop thy bleating,' says Tom. 'Stand quiet a moment. Let's draw the exe out of thy body, and I'll give thee a chance for another round. Thee doesn't deserve it, because thee aren't playing fair.'

Tom turned the giant over, laid hold of the wheel, and dragged out the 'exe'. In doing this he was nearly blinded with the blood that spouted out of the hole. Blunderbuss rolled on the ground like an empty sack, roaring amain all the time in great agony.

'Stop thy bleating,' says Tom, 'and put thy hands in the hole the exe has made in thee, to keep in the blood, until I can cut a turf to stop up the place, and thee will'st do again yet.'

As Tom was plugging the wound with the turfs, the giant groaned and said, 'It's all no good; I shall kick the bucket. I feel myself going round land; but with my last breath I'll do thee good, because I like thee better than anybody else I ever met with, for thy fair play and courage. The more thee wouldst beat me, the better I should like thee. I have no near relations. There is heaps of gold, silver, copper, and tin down in the vaults of the castle, guarded by two dogs. Mind their names are Catchem and Tearem. Only call them by these names and they'll let thee pass. The land from this to the sea is all mine. There is more head of oxen, cows, sheep, goats, and deer, than thee canst count. Take them all, only bury me decent.'

'Did you kill all your wives?' asked Tom.

'No,' sighed the giant, 'they died natural. Don't let them abuse me after death. I like thee as a brother.'

'Cheer up,' says Tom, 'you'll do again.'

He then tried to raise the giant up, but the plug of turf slipped from the wound, and all was over.

Tom put the wheel and axle in order, turned over the wain, and drove home to Market-Jew. The brewer was surprised and well pleased to see Tom back so early, and offered him good wages to stop for the year.

'I must leave this very night,' says Tom, 'for my old granfer, who lived up in the high countries, is dead. I am his nearest relation. He lived all alone. He's left me all his money and lands, so I must go and bury my old granfer this very night.' The brewer was about to pay him for his day's work – 'Oh, never mind that,' says Tom; 'I'll give up that for as much beer as I can drink with supper.'

After supper Tom went and took possession of the giant's castle and lands – nobody the wiser except a little woman, the giant's last wife, who came from some place not far from the castle.

Some name Crowlas, some Tregender, others Bougiehere, as the place where she dwelt. Howbeit, she knew all about the giant's overthrow, and thought it the wisest course to 'take up' at once with Tom; and she being a tidy body, Tom was by no means unwilling. Tom and this woman took possession of the castle.

They buried the giant down in the bottom, and placed a block of granite to keep him down. They gave the carcass of a sheep to Catchem and Tearem, visited the caves of the castle, found lots of treasure, and fairly got into the giant's shoes.

Tom the Giant, his wife Jane, and Jack the Tinkeard, as told by the 'Drolls'

When Tom and his wife had settled themselves in the giant's castle, they took good care not to allow any one to make a king's highway across their grounds. Tom made the hedges higher, and the gates stronger than ever, and he claimed all the run of land on the sea-side, and enclosed it. Tom's wife, Jane, was a wonderful cleanly body – the castle seemed to be always fresh swept and sanded, while all the pewter plates and platters shone like silver. She never quarrelled with Tom, except when he came in from hedging covered with mud; then in a pet she would threaten to go home to her mother.

Jane was very famous for her butter and cheese, and Tom became no less so for his fine breed of cattle, so that he fared luxuriously, and all went on happily enough with Tom and his wife. They had plenty of children, and these were such fine healthy babies, that it took two or three of the best cows to feed them, when but a few weeks old. Tom and Jane thought that they had all that part of the world to themselves, and that no one could scale their hedges or break through their gates. They soon found their mistake. Tom was working one morning, not far from the gate, on the Market-Jew side of his property, when he heard a terrible rattle upon the bars. Running up, he saw a man with a hammer smashing away, and presently down went the bars, and in walked a travelling tinkeard, with his bag of tools on his back.

'Holla! where are you bound for?' says Tom.

'Bound to see if the giant, who they say lives up here, wouldn't let a body pass through where the road ought to be,' says the tinkeard.

'Oh, ay! are you?' says Tom.

'He must be a better man than I am who stops me,' says the tinkeard. 'As you are a fine stout chap, I expect you are the giant's eldest son. I see you are hedging. That 's what all the people complain of. You are hedging in all the country.'

'Well,' says Tom, 'if I am his son, I can take my dad's part anyway; and we'll have fair play too. I don't desire better fun than to try my strength with somebody that is a man. Come on. Any way you like – naked fists, single-stick, wrestling, bowling, slinging, or throwing the quoits.'

'Very well,' says the tinkeard, 'I'll match my blackthorn stick against anything in the way of timber that you can raise on this place.'

Tom took the bar which the tinker had broken from the gate, and said, 'I'll try this piece of elm if you don't think it too heavy.'

'Don't care if it's heavier. Come on!'

The tinkeard took the thorn-stick in the middle, and made it fly round Tom's head so fast that he couldn't see it. It looked like a wheel whizzing round his ears, and Tom soon got a bloody nose and two black eyes. Tom's blows had no effect on the tinkeard, because he wore such a coat as was never seen in the West Country before. It was made out of a shaggy black bull's hide, dressed whole with the hair on. The skin of the forelegs made the sleeves, the hind quarters only were cut, pieces being let in to make the spread of the skirts, while the neck and skin of the head formed a sort of hood. The whole appeared as hard as iron; and when Tom hit the tinkeard, it sounded as if the coat roared, like thunder. They fought until Tom got very hungry, and he found he had the worst of it. 'I believe thee art the devil, and no man,' says Tom. 'Let's see thy feet before thee dost taste any more of my blood.'

The tinkeard showed Tom that he had no cloven foot, and told him that it depended more on handiness than strength to conquer with the single-stick; and that a small man with science could beat a big man with none. The tinkeard then took the clumsy bar of the gate from Tom, gave him his own light and tough blackthorn, and proceeded to teach him to make the easiest passes, cuts, etc.

Whilst the two men were thus engaged, Jane had prepared the dinner, and called her husband three times. She wondered what could be keeping Tom, as he was always ready to run to his dinner at the first call. At length she went out of the castle to seek for him, and surprised she was, and – if truth must be told – rather glad to see another man inside the gates, which no one had passed for years. Jane found Tom and the tinkeard tolerable friends by this time, and she begged them both to come in to dinner, saying to the tinkeard that she wished she had something better to set before him. She was vexed that Tom hadn't sent her word, that she might have prepared something better than the everlasting beef and pease; and vowed she would give him a more savoury mess for supper, if she had to go to the hills for a sheep or a kid herself.

At length the men were seated at the board, which groaned beneath the huge piece of boiled beef, with mountains of pease-pudding, and they soon got fairly to work. Jane then went to the cellar, and tapped a barrel of the strongest beer, which was intended to have been kept for a tide (feast). Of the meat, Tom ate twice as much as the tinkeard, and from the can of ale he took double draughts. The tinkeard ate heartily, but not voraciously; and, for those days, he was no hard drinker.

Consequently, as soon as dinner was over, Tom fell back against the wall, and was quickly snoring like a tempest. His custom was to sleep two or three hours after every meal. The tinkeard was no sleepy-head, so he told Jane to bring him all her pots and pans which required mending, and he would put them in order. He seated himself amidst a vast pile, and was soon at work. The louder Tom snored, the more Jack rattled and hammered away at the kettles; and ere Tom was awake, he had restored Jane's cooking vessels to something like condition.

At length Tom awoke, and, feeling very sore, he begged the tinkeard to put off until to-morrow a wrestling-match which they had talked of before dinner. The tinkeard, nothing loath, agreed; so Tom took him up to the topmost tower of the castle, to show him his lands and his cattle. For miles and miles, farther over the hill than the eye could reach, except on the southern side, everything belonged to Tom. In this tower they found a long and strong bow. Tom said none but the old giant could bend it. He had often tried, and fretted because he could not bring the string to the notch. The tinkeard took the bow; he placed one end to his toe, and, by what appeared like sleight-of-hand to Tom, he bent the bow, brought the string to the notch, sent the arrow off – thwang – and shot a hare so far away that it could hardly be seen from the heath and ferns. Tom was surprised, until the tinkeard showed him how to bend the bow, more by handiness than strength, and again he killed a kid which was springing from rock to rock on the cairns far away. The hare and kid were brought home, cooked for supper, and the tinkeard was invited to stop all night.

The story ordinarily rambles on, telling of the increasing friendship between the three, and giving the tinkeard's story of himself, which was so interesting to Tom and Jane that they stayed up nearly all night to hear it. He told how he was born and bred in a country far away – more than a score days' journey from this land, far to the north and east of this, from which it was divided by a large river. This river the tinkeard had swum across; then there was a week's journey in a land of hills and cairns, which were covered with snow a great part of the year. In this land there were many giants, who digged for tin and other treasures.

With these giants he had lived and worked – they always treated him well; indeed, he always found the bigger the man the more gentle. Half the evil that's told about them by the cowardly fools who fear to go near them is false. Many, many more strange things did the tinkeard tell. Amongst other matters, he spoke of wise men who came from a city at no great distance from this land of tin for the purpose of buying the tin from the giants, and they left them tools, and other things, that the diggers required in exchange. One of these merchants took a fancy to the tinkeard, named him Jack – he had no name previously – and removed him to the city, where Jack was taught his trade, and many other crafts. The tinkeard had left that city four months since, and worked his way down to Market-Jew. Being there, he heard of the giant, and he resolved to make his acquaintance. The rest has been told.

While this, which was a long story, was being told, Jack the Tinkeard was enjoying Jane's new barley-bread, with honey and cream, which he moistened with metheglin. 'Good night, Tom,' says he at last; 'you see you have lived all your days like a lord on his lands, and know nothing. I never knew father or mother, never had a home to call my own. All the better for me, too. If I had possessed one, I would never have known one-thousandth part of what I have learned by wandering up and down in the world.'

Morning came; and, after breakfast, Tom proposed to try 'a hitch' on the grass in the castle court. Jack knew nothing of wrestling; so he told Tom he had never practised, but still he would try his strength. Tom put the tinkeard on his back at every 'hitch', but he took all the care he could not to hurt him. At last the tinkeard cried for quarter, and declared Tom to be best man.

Jane had made a veal-and-parsley pie, and put it down to bake, when, being at leisure, she came out to see the sport. Now, it must be remembered the tinkeard had broken down the gate, and no one had thought of repairing it, or closing the opening. Two men of Tregender were coming home from bal, and passing the giant's gate, they thought it very strange that it should be broken down. After consulting for some time, they summoned all their courage, and – it must be confessed, with fear and trembling – they crawled into the grounds, and proceeded towards the castle. Now, no one in that country except Tom and Jane knew that the old giant was dead.

The two men turned round a corner, and saw three very large children playing. The baby, a year old, was riding an old buck-goat about the field. The two elder children, Tom Vean and young Jane, were mounted on a bull, back to back, one holding on by the horns, and the other by the tail, galloping round the field like mad, followed by the cows and dogs – a regular 'cow's courant'.

'Lord, you,' says one of the men to the other, 'what dost a' think of that for a change?'

'But to think,' says the other, 'that the old giant should ever have a wife and young chil'ren here, and the people knaw nothing about it.'

'Why, don't everybody say that he ate all his wives and children too. What lies people tell, don't they, you?'

'Let's go a little farther; he won't eat we, I suppose.'

'I'll throw my pick and sho'el down the throat of an, as soon as a'do open as [his] jaws.'

'Look you,' now shouts the other, 'you come round a little farther: just peep round the corner and thee meest see two fellows wrestling, and a woman looking on.'

'Can I believe my eyes, you? Don't that woman look something like Jane I used to be courson of?'

The miners satisfied themselves that it was Jane, sure enough, and quietly beat a retreat. Soon was St Ives in a state of excitement, and all Jane's cousins, believing from the accounts given by the miners that Jane was well off, resolved to pay her a visit. These visits worked much confusion in Tom's castle and family. He and his wife quarrel, but the tinkeard is the never-failing friend.

All this part of the story is an uninteresting account of fair-weather friends. Jack the Tinkeard taught Tom how to till his ground in a proper manner. He had hitherto contented himself with gathering wild herbs – such as nettles, wild beet, mallows, elecampane, various kinds of lentils, and chick or cat-peas. Jack now planted a garden for his friends – the first in Cornwall – and they grew all kinds of good vegetables. The tinkeard also taught Jane to make malt and to brew beer; hitherto they had been content with barley-wort, which was often sour.

Jack would take the children and collect bitter herbs to make the beer keep, such as the alehoof (ground ivy), mugwort, bannell (the broom), agrimony, centaury, wood-sage, bettony, and pellitory. Jane's beer was now amongst the choicest of drinks, and her St Ives cousins could never have enough of it. Tom delighted in it, and often drank enough to bewilder his senses.

Tom had followed the example of the old giant, and killed his cattle by flinging rocks at them. The giant's 'bowls' are seen to this day scattered all over the country. Jack gave Tom a knife of the keenest edge and finest temper, and taught him how to slaughter the beasts. When a calf was to be skinned, he instructed Tom how to take the skin off whole from the fore legs, by unjointing the shoulders, and to remove it entirely clear of grain, and without the smallest scratch.

In addition to all this, Tommy Vean (who was now a boy four years old, but bigger than many at ten) must have a coat possessing all the virtues which belonged to the tinkeard's. So a bull-calf's skin was put on to the boy, and Jane had special instructions how she was to allow the coat to dry on his back, and tan and dress it in a peculiar way. The skin thus treated would shrink and thicken up until it came to his shape. Nobody can tell how proud the young Tom was of his coat when all was done, though the poor boy suffered much in the doing.

Now Jack the Tinkeard desired the intrusion of strangers as little as did Tom and Jane, so he set to work to repair the gate which he had broken down. He not only did this, but he constructed a curious latch with the bobbin; it was so contrived that no stranger could find the right end of it, and if they pulled at any other part, the latch was only closed the tighter. While he was at work a swarm of Jane's St Ives cousins came around him; they mistook Jack for Tom, and pointed out how the children, who were playing near him, were like their father. Jack 'parlayed' with them until he had completed his task, and then he closed the gate in their faces.

Much more of this character is related by the 'drolls'; but with the exception of constant alternations of feasting and fighting, there is little of novelty in the story, until at last a grand storm arises between Tom and his wife, who is believed by the husband to be on too intimate terms with Jack the Tinkeard.

The result of this is, that Jane goes home to Crowlas, fights with her mother, old Jenny, because old Jenny abuses Tom, which Jane will not allow in her presence. While yet at Crowlas another boy is born, called Honey; and, as the cow was not at hand as when she was in the castle, he was nursed by a goat, and it is said a class of his descendants are yet known as the Zennor goats.

How Tom and the Tinkeard found the tin, and how it led to Morvah Fair

When Tom had fairly thrown the tinkeard in the wrestling match, which, it must be remembered, was seen by the miners of Tregender, at which Tom was much pleased, although he did not express his pleasure, it was settled that Tom was the best man. This was sealed over a barrel of strong ale, and a game of quoits was proposed, while Jane was taking up the dinner. Tom had often wished, but never more so than now, that the green sloping banks against the inside of the castle walls had not been there, that he might have a fair fling of the quoits from end to end of the court. Tom's third throw in this game was a very strong one, and the quoit cut a great piece of turf from the banks, laying bare many grey-looking stones, small rounded balls, and black sandy stuff.

'Look here you, Jack,' says Tom, 'whatever could possess the old fools of giants to heap up such a lot of black and grey mining-stones against the wall? Wherever could they have found them all?'

Jack carefully looked at the stuff thus laid bare, clapped his hands together, and shouted 'By the gods, it's all the richest tin!'

Now Tom, poor easy-going soul, 'didn't knaw tin', so he could scarcely believe Jack, though Jack had told him that he came from a tin country.

'Why, Tom,' says Jack, ' thee art a made man. If these banks are all tin, there is enough here to buy all the land, and all the houses, from sea to sea.'

'What do I care for the tin; haven't I all a man can desire? My lands are all stocked with sheep and horned cattle. We shall never lack the best beef and mutton, and we want no better than our honest homespun.'

Jane now made her appearance, announcing that dinner was

ready. She was surprised at seeing so much tin, but she didn't say anything. She thought maybe she would get a new gown out of it, and go down to St Ives Fair. Notwithstanding that Tom and Jane professed to treat lightly the discovery of the tin, it was clear they thought deeply about it, and their thoughts spoiled their appetites. It was evidently an accession of wealth which they could not understand.

Tom said he didn't know how to dress tin, it was of little use to him. Jack offered to dress it for the market on shares. Tom told him he might take as much as he had a mind to for what he cared. After dinner, the giant tried to sleep, but could not get a snore for the soul of him. Therefore, he walked out into the court, to get some fresh air, as he said, but in reality to look at the tin. Jane saw how restless Tom was, so she unhung his bows and arrows, and told him he must away to the hills to get some kids and hares.

'I shan't trouble myself with the bows and arrows,' says Tom; 'all I want are the slings Jack and I have in our pockets. Stones are plenty enough, hit or miss, no matter; and we needn't be at the trouble to gather up the stones again.'

Off went Tom and Jack, followed by young Tom and Jane, to the Towednack and Zennor hills. They soon knocked down as many kids, hares, and rabbits as they desired – they caught some colts, placed the children on two of them and the game on the others, and home they went. On their return, whilst waiting for supper, Jack wandered around the castle, and was struck by seeing a window which he had not before observed. Jack was resolved to discover the room to which this window belonged, so he very carefully noticed its position, and then threw his hammer in through it, that he might be certain of the spot when he found the tool inside the castle.

The next day, after dinner, when Tom was having his snooze, Jack took Jane with him, and they commenced a search for the hammer near the spot where Jack supposed the window should be, but they saw no signs of one in in any part of the walls. They discovered, however, a strangely-fashioned, worm-eaten oak hanging-press. They carefully examined this, but found nothing.

At last Jack, striking the back of it with his fist, was convinced, from the sound, that the wall behind it was hollow. He and Jane went steadily to work, and with some exertion they moved the press aside, and disclosed a stone door. They opened this, and there was Jack's hammer lying amidst a pile of bones, evidently the relics of some of old Blunderbuss's wives, whom he had imprisoned in the wall, and who had perished there. Jane was in a great fright, and blessed her good fortune that she had escaped a similar end.

Jack, however, soon consoled her by showing her the splendid dresses which were here, and the gold chains, rings, and bracelets, with diamonds and other jewels, which were scattered around. It was agreed that Tom for the present should be kept in ignorance of all this. Tom awoke, his head full of the tin. He consulted with Jack and Jane. They duly agreed to keep their secret, and resolved that they would set to work the very next day to prepare some of the tin stuff for sale. Tom as yet scarcely believed in his wealth, which was magnified as much as possible by Jack, to bewilder him. However, several sacks of tin were duly dressed, and Tom and Jack started with them for Market-Jew, Tom whispering to Jack before he left the castle, that they would bring home a cask of the brewer's best ale with 'em. 'It is a lot better than what Jane brews with her old-fashioned yerbes; but don't ye tell her so.'

The brewer of Market-Jew was also mayor, and, as it appears, tin-smelter, or tin merchant. To him, therefore, Tom went with his black tin, and received not only his cask of beer, but such an amount of golden coin – all of it being a foreign coinage – as convinced him that Jack had not deceived him.

This brewer is reputed to have been an exceedingly honest and kind-hearted man, beloved by all. It was his practice, when any of the townspeople came before him, begging him to settle their disputes – even when they 'limbed' one another – to shut them up in the brewery-yard, give them as much beer as they could drink, and keep them there until they became good friends.

Owing to this practice he seldom had enough beer to sell, and was frequently troubled to pay for his barley. This brewer, who was reputed to be 'the best mayor that ever was since the creation of grey cats', gave rise, from the above practice of his, to the proverb still in daily use, 'Standing, like the mayor of Market-Jew, in his own light.'

The mayor was always fat and jolly. He was an especial favourite, too, with the Lord of Pengersick, who is believed to have helped him out of many troubles. He had bought his tin of Tom and Jack, such a bargain, that he resolved to have some sport, so a barrel of beer was broached in the yard, and the crier was sent round the town to call all hands to a 'courant' (merry-making). They came, you may be certain, in crowds. There was wrestling, hurling – the length of the Green from Market-Jew to Chyandour, and back again – throwing quoits, and slinging.

Some amused themselves in pure wantonness by slinging stones over the Mount; so that the old giant, who lived there, was afraid to show above ground, lest his only eye should get knocked out.

The games were kept up right merrily until dusk, when in rode the Lord of Pengersick on his enchanted mare, with a colt by her side. The brewer introduced Tom and Jack, and soon they became the best of friends. Tom invited Pengersick to his castle, and they resolved to go home at once and make a night of it. Pengersick gave Tom the colt, and, by some magic power, as soon as he mounted this beautiful animal, he found himself at home, and the lord, the brewer, and Jack with him. How this was brought about Tom could never tell, but Jack appeared to be in the secret. Tom was amazed and delighted to find Jane dressed like a queen, in silks and diamonds, and the children arrayed in a manner well becoming the dignity of their mother.

Jane, as soon as Tom and Jack had left her, had proceeded to the room in the wall, and with much care removed the jewels, gold, and dresses, caring little, as she afterwards said, for the dead bones, although they rattled as she shook them out of the robes. In a little time she had all the dresses in the main court of the castle, and having well beaten and brushed them, she selected the finest – those she now wore – and put the rest aside for other grand occasions.

The condescension of the great Lord of Pengersick was something wonderful. He kissed Jane until Tom was almost jealous, and the great lord romped about the court of the castle with the children. Tom was, on the whole however, delighted with the attention paid to his wife by a real lord, but our clear-headed Jack saw through it all, and took measures accordingly.

Pengersick tried hard to learn the secret of the stores of tin, but he was foiled by the tinkeard on every tack. You may well suppose how desirous he was of getting Jack out of the way, and eventually he began to try his spells upon him.

The power of his necromancy was such, that all in the castle were fixed in sleep as rigid as stones, save Jack. All that the enchanter could do produced no effect on him. He sat quietly looking on, occasionally humming some old troll, and now and then whistling to show his unconcern. At last Pengersick became enraged, and he drew from his breast a dagger and slyly struck at Jack. The dagger, which was of the finest Eastern steel, was bent like a piece of soft iron against Jack's black hide.

'Art thou the devil?' exclaimed Pengersick.

'As he's a friend of yours,' says Jack, 'you should know his countenance.'

'Devil or no devil,' roared Pengersick, 'you cannot resist this,' and he held before Jack a curiously-shaped piece of polished steel.

Jack only smiled, and quietly unfastening his cow's hide, he opened it. The cross, like a star of fire, was reflected in a mirror under Jack's coat, and it fell from Pengersick's grasp. Jack seized it, and turning it full upon the enchanter, the proud lord sank trembling to the ground, piteously imploring Jack to spare his life and let him go free. Jack bade the prostrate lord rise from the ground.

He kicked him out of the castle, and sent the vicious mare after him. Thus he saved Tom and his family from the power of this great enchanter. In a little time the sleep which had fallen upon them passed away, and they awoke, as though from the effects of a drunken frolic. The brewer hurried home, and Tom and Jack set to work to dress their tin.

Tom and Jane's relations and friends flocked around them, but Jack said, 'Summer flies are only seen in the sunshine,' and he shortly after this put their friendship to the test, by conveying to them the idea that Tom had spent all his wealth. These new friends dropped off when they thought they could get no more, and Tom and Jane were thoroughly disgusted with their summer friends and selfish relations. The tinkeard established himself firmly as an inmate of the castle. No more was said about the right of the public to make a king's highway through the castle grounds. He aided Tom in hedging in the waste lands, and very carefully secured the gates against all intruders. In fact, he also quite altered his politics.

Jack had a desire to go home to Dartmoor to see his mother, who had sent to tell him that the old giant Dart was near death. He started at once, on foot. Tom wished him to have Pengersick's colt, but Jack preferred his legs. It would be too long a tale to tell the story of his travels. He killed serpents and wild beasts in the woods, and when he came to rivers, he had but to take off his coat, gather up the skirts of it with a string, and stretch out the body with a few sticks – thus forming a coble – launch it on the water, and paddle himself across. He reached home. The old giant was at his last gasp. Jack made him give everything to his mother before he breathed his last. When he died, Jack carefully buried him. He then settled all matters for his mother, and returned to the West Country again.

Tom's daughter became of marriageable years, and Jack wished to have her for a wife. Tom, however, would not consent to this, unless he got rid of a troublesome old giant who lived on one of the hills in Morvah, which was the only bit of ground between Hayle and St Just which Tom did not possess.

The people of Morvah were kept in great fear by this giant, who made them bring him the best of everything. He was a very savage old creature, and took exceeding delight in destroying everyone's happiness. Some of Tom's cousins lived in Morvah, and young Tom fell in love with one of his Morvah cousins seven times removed, and by Jack's persuasion, they were allowed by Tom and Jane to marry.

It was proclaimed by Jack all round the country that great games would come off on the day of the wedding. He had even the impudence to stick a bill on the giant's door, stating the prizes which would be given to the best games. The happy day arrived, and, as the custom then was, the marriage was to take place at sundown. A host of people from all parts were assembled, and under the influence of Jack and Tom, the games were kept up in great spirit.

Jack and Tom, by and by, amused themselves by pitching quoits at the giant's house on the top of the hill. The old giant came out and roared like thunder. All the young men were about to fly, but Jack called them a lot of scurvy cowards, and stayed their flight. Jack made faces at the giant, and challenged him to come down and fight him. The old monster thought he could eat Jack, and presently began to run down the hill – when, lo! he disappeared. When the people saw that the giant was gone, they took courage, and ran up the hill after Jack, who called on them to follow him.

There was a vast hole in the earth, and there, at the bottom of it, lay the giant, crushed by his own weight, groaning like a volcano and shaking like an earthquake.

Jack knew there was an adit level driven into the hill, and he had quietly, and at night, worked away the roof at one particular part, until he left only a mere shell of rock above, so it was, that, as the giant passed over this spot, the ground gave way. Heavy rocks were thrown down the hole on the giant, and there his bones are said to lie to this day.

Jack was married at once to young Jane, her brother Tom to the Morvah girl, and great were the rejoicings. From all parts of the country came in the wrestlers, and never since the days of Gogmagog had there been such terrific struggles between strong men. Quoits were played; and some of the throws of Tom and the tinkeard are still shown to attest the wonderful prowess of this pair. Hurling was played over the wild hills of those northern shores, and they rung and echoed then, as they have often rung and echoed since, with the brave cry, 'Guare wheag yw guare teag' which has been translated into 'Fair play is good play' – an honourable trait in the character of our Celtic friends.

All this took place on a Sunday, and was the origin of Morvah Feast and Morvah Fair. We are, of course, astonished at not finding some evidence of direct punishment for these offences, such as that which was inflicted on the hurlers at Padstow. This has, however, been explained on the principle that the people were merely rejoicing at the accomplishment of a most holy act, and that a good deed demanded a good day.

The Giant of Morvah

In the Giant's Field in Morvah still stand some granite fragments which once constituted the Giant's House. From this we see the Giant's Castle at Bosprenis, and the Giant's Cradle, thus perpetuating the infancy of the great man, and his subsequent power. The quoits used by this giant are numerous indeed. This great man, on the 1st day of August, would walk up to Bosprenis Croft, and there perform some magical rites, which were either never known, or they have been forgotten. On this day – for when thus engaged the giant was harmless – thousands of people would congregate to get a glimpse of the monster; and as he passed them – all being seated on the stone hedges – every one drank 'to the health of Mr Giant'. At length the giant died, but the gathering on the 1st of August has never been given up, or rather, the day shifts, and is made to agree with Morvah Feast, which is held on the first Sunday in August.

A Morvah farmer writes: 'A quarter of an acre would not hold the horses ridden to the fair – the hedges being covered by the visitors, who drink and carouse as in former times.'

The parish-clerk informed me that the giant had twenty sons; that he was the first settler in these parts; and that he planted his children all round the coast. It was his custom to bring all his family together on the 1st of August, and hence the origin of the fair. Whichever may be the true account of the cause which established the fair and the feast, these romances clearly establish the fact that the giants were at the bottom of it.

The Giant Bolster

This mighty man held especial possession of the hill formerly known as Carne Bury-anacht or Bury-anack 'the spar-stone grave', which is now named, from the use made of the hill during the long war, St Agnes Beacon. He has left his name to a very interesting, and undoubtedly most ancient earthwork, which still exists at the base of the hill, and evidently extended from Trevaunance Porth to Chapel Porth, enclosing the most important tin district in St Agnes. This is constantly called 'The Bolster'.

Bolster must have been of enormous size, since it is stated that he could stand with one foot on St Agnes Beacon and the other on Carn Brea; these hills being distant, as the bird flies, six miles, this immensity will be clear to all. In proof of this, there still exists, in the valley running upwards from Chapel Porth, a stone in which may yet be seen the impression of the giant's fingers.

On one occasion, Bolster, when enjoying his usual stride from the Beacon to Carn Brea, felt thirsty, and stooped to drink out of the well at Chapel Porth, resting, while he did so, on the above-mentioned stone. We hear but little of the wives of our giants, but Bolster had a wife, who was made to labour hard by her tyrannical husband.

On the top of St Agnes Beacon there yet exist the evidences of the useless labours to which this unfortunate giantess was doomed, in grouped masses of small stones. These, it is said, have all been gathered from an estate at the foot of the hill, immediately adjoining the village of St Agnes. This farm is to the present day remarkable for its freedom from stones, though situated amidst several others, which, like most lands reclaimed from the moors of this district, have stones in abundance mixed with the soil.

Whenever Bolster was angry with his wife, he compelled her to pick stones, and to carry them in her apron to the top of the hill. There is some confusion in the history of this giant, and of the blessed St Agnes to whom the church is dedicated. They are supposed to have lived at the same time, which, according to our views, is scarcely probable, believing, as we do, that no giants existed long after their defeat at Plymouth by Brutus and Corineus. There may have been an earlier saint of the same name; or may not Saint Enns or Anns, the popular name of this parish, indicate some other lady?

Be this as it may, the giant Bolster became deeply in love with St Agnes, who is reputed to have been singularly beautiful, and a pattern woman of virtue. The giant allowed the lady no repose. He followed her incessantly, proclaiming his love, and filling the air with the tempests of his sighs and groans.

St Agnes lectured Bolster in vain on the impropriety of his conduct, he being already a married man. This availed not; her prayers to him to relieve her from his importunities were also in vain. The persecuted lady, finding there was no release for her, while this monster existed, resolved to be rid of him at any cost, and eventually succeeded by the following stratagem: Agnes appeared at length to be persuaded of the intensity of the giant's love, but she told him she required yet one small proof more. There exists at Chapel Porth a hole in the cliff at the termination of the valley. If Bolster would fill this hole with his blood the lady would no longer look coldly on him.

This huge bestrider-of-the-hills thought that it was an easy thing which was required of him, and felt that he could fill many such holes and be none the weaker for the loss of blood. Consequently, stretching his great arm across the hole, he plunged a knife into a vein, and a torrent of gore issued forth. Roaring and seething the blood fell to the bottom, and the giant expected in a few minutes to see the test of his devotion made evident, in the filling of the hole.

It required much more blood than Bolster had supposed; still it must in a short time be filled, so he bled on. Hour after hour the blood flowed from the vein yet the hole was not filled. Eventually the giant fainted from exhaustion. The strength of life within his mighty frame enabled him to rally, yet he had no power to lift himself from the ground, and he was unable to stanch the wound which he had made. Thus it was, that after many throes, the giant Bolster died!

The cunning saint, in proposing this task to Bolster, was well aware that the hole opened at the bottom into the sea, and that as rapidly as the blood flowed into the hole it ran from it, and did

The multitudinous seas incarnadine,
Making the green one red.

Thus the lady got rid of her hated lover; Mrs Bolster was released, and the district freed from the presence of a tyrant. The hole at Chapel Porth still retains the evidences of the truth of this tradition, in the red stain which marks the track down which flowed the giant's blood.

There is another tradition, in some respects resembling this one, respecting a giant who dwelt at Goran, on the south coast.

The Hack and Cast

In the parish of Goran is an intrenchment running from cliff to cliff, and cutting off about a hundred acres of coarse ground. This is about twenty feet broad, and twenty-four feet high in most places.

Marvellous as it may appear, tradition assures us that this was the work of a giant, and that he performed the task in a single night. This fortification has long been known as Thica Vosa, and the Hack and Cast.

The giant, who lived on the promontory, was the terror of the neighbourhood, and great were the rejoicings in Goran when his death was accomplished through a stratagem by a neighbouring doctor. The giant fell ill through eating some food – children or otherwise – to satisfy his voracity, which had disturbed his stomach. His roars and groans were heard for miles, and great was the terror throughout the neighbourhood.

A messenger, however, soon arrived at the residence of the doctor of the parish, and he bravely resolved to obey the summons of the giant, and visit him. He found the giant rolling on the ground with pain, and he at once determined to rid the world, if possible, of the monster.

He told him that he must be bled. The giant submitted, and the doctor moreover said that, to insure relief, a large hole in the cliff must be filled with the blood. The giant lay on the ground, his arm extended over the hole, and the blood flowing a torrent into it. Relieved by the loss of blood, he permitted the stream to flow on, until he at last became so weak, that the doctor kicked him over the cliff, and killed him.

The well-known promontory of The Dead Man, or Dodman, is so called from the dead giant. The spot on which he fell is the 'Giant's House', and the hole has ever since been most favourable to the growth of ivy.